HOW TO
DRESS
RICH

Dale Goday
with
Monique Ross

PRINCIPAL PHOTOGRAPHY BY
JOEL BRODSKY

A FIRESIDE BOOK
Published by Simon and Schuster
New York

Copyright © 1982 by Symphony Press
All rights reserved
including the right of reproduction
in whole or in part in any form
A Fireside Book
Published by Simon and Schuster
A Division of Gulf & Western Corporation
Simon & Schuster Building
Rockefeller Center
1230 Avenue of the Americas
New York, New York 10020
FIRESIDE and colophon are registered trademarks of Simon &
Schuster.
Designed by Elaine Golt Gongora
Manufactured in the United States of America
Printed and bound by Semline, Inc.
10   9   8   7   6   5   4   3   2   1
Library of Congress Cataloging in Publication Data
Goday, Dale.
    How to dress rich.
    "A Fireside book."
    1. Clothing and dress.   2. Fashion.   I. Ross,
Monique.   II. Title.
TT507.G583   1982   646'.34   82-16791
ISBN: 0-671-45334-3

Acknowledgments

Many thanks to the following people whose talent and support made *How to Dress Rich* a reality:

To Joel Brodsky, whose photography brought the concept to life.

And to Val Brodsky, for all the help she so generously offered.

And a very special thanks to Gaye Lakin for her dedication, styling input, fashion expertise, and especially her friendship.

Our appreciation to Ian Fulton for his dedication and hard work.

With sincere gratitude to
Hunan Wok for their prompt
deliveries of those wonderfully
delicious little white boxes.

Contents

Credits

Joel Brodsky's photographs appear on the cover and pages 10, 14, 15, 16, 17, 23, 26, 29, 33, 43, 44, 46, 48, 49, 54, 57, 60, 61, 72, 99, 107.

Blassport—photography by Gideon Lewin: pages 100 and 108.

Bottega Veneta: pages 103 and 104.

Joel Brodsky—Vogue Patterns: pages 84, 85, 87, 91, 92, 94.

Courtesy of Burberrys: page 63.

Courtesy of Butterick Patterns: pages 21, 51, 54, 68, 69, 70, 76, 77, 78, 82.

Courtesy of Gottex: pages 64, 65, 66.

Courtesy of Calvin Klein: pages 39 and 55.

Courtesy of Pierre Michel: pages 24 and 25.

Jack Mulqueen: pages 18 and 72.

Courtesy of Albert Nipon: pages 53 and 58.

Models: (in order of appearance)

Alicia Munn-Sue Charney agency
Barbara Fines-Sue Charney agency
Cindy Reynolds-Sue Charney agency (also on cover)
Deborah Carroll-Sue Charney agency
Clarke Harison-Sue Charney agency
Laura Jones-Ford agency
Janice Soukup-Sue Charney agency
Jennifer Ivey-Sue Charney agency
Donna Geis-Wilhelmina agency

Hair Styling and Makeup:
Ted Buckwald
Frederique

Researchers:
Betsy Jablow
Enid Klass

General Assistance:
Lea Sigiel, Jennifer Reek, Paul Duffy, Rich Calve

Clothing on cover:
J. G. Hook

This book would not have been possible without the coopera-
tion of the following manufacturers, designers, stores, and
good friends:

Harvé Benard
Ted Berkowitz
Bis
Bill Blass Hats
Blassport
Donna Bulseco
Burberry
Butterick Patterns
Cabal
Marisa Christina
Columbia Handkerchief &
   Accessory Co.
Linda Connely
Oscar de la Renta Knits
Design Observations
Madeline de Uries
Bonnie Doon
Dupont
Electric Sok
Carlos Falchi
The Footwear Council
Adriana Fosi
Gottex
Hanky Panky
Hat Hospital
Nancy Heller

J. G. Hook
Kenar
Kenneth J. Lane Jewelry
Mercura
Pierre Michel
Mirage
Jack Mulqueen, Ltd.
National Handbag Association
Albert Nipon
Our Favorite Things
Rod Owens
Parabe Furs
Putumayo
Prelude
Peter Rogers Associates
S&W Stores
Louise Sams
Savage
Jill Stuart Belts
Swing Low
Terra
Ellen Tracy
Chris Varone
Vera Scarfs
Vogue Patterns
Jane Wheatley

Introduction

You see it when you leaf through *Town And Country* in those candid shots of Prince and Princess Von So-and-So standing around with Astors or Rothschilds or Fords in the endless backyard of someone's sprawling Newport mansion.

You see it in Southampton while looking for a nut to fit a bolt in Fertig's Hardware Store.

You see it at the bar at the Ritz Carlton in Chicago, at dinner at Chasen's in Beverly Hills, at the horse show in Houston, and even sometimes when buying a copy of *TV Guide* at your local candy store.

The Rich Look. Basically, it comes in two forms— Classic and High Fashion (and sometimes a mixture of the two). But whatever the interpretation, the look is unmistakable and often sublime. Our recognition of it is instantaneous, our reaction one of awe. For without our quite understanding how she's done it, we see before us a woman whose aura is at once attractive, formidable, superior, charismatic, self-assured, and not without a certain sex appeal.

How come I never look like that? we wonder. How does she do it? What are the ingredients?

Opposite: The High Fashion yet Classic "little black dress" accessorized with forsade choker pearls, gold bangle, and black sheer stockings. Hair is worn in the ever classic chignon. Attractive. Charismatic. Sublime.

11

But before we can finish taking apart her wardrobe piece by piece, we give up. Our mind becomes a muddle. Why bother? Even if we could figure out the formula, who could ever afford the ingredients?

You can. Oh, sure, the Rich Look *can* cost a fortune. But it doesn't necessarily have to. If taken apart and studied and *understood*, you can put it all together for considerably less than a fortune . . . in fact for about the same as you're spending on clothes right now.

So let's begin. This is not to say you want to put on the Rich Look everyday. Sometimes nothing is more fun than rousting about in the garden in a pair of Sears dungarees and the oversized orange tee shirt your husband got for running in the Hackensack Mini-Marathon.

But then there are those other times—your college reunion, the weekend at your boss's estate at the shore—when for once *you'd* like to be the one who everyone else stops to look at because you appear so superior and self-assured.

1

Choosing Your Look

There are basically two rich looks from which you can choose: High Fashion and Classic. The two styles of dress are distinctly different, yet all the important fashion statements and trends can be found in both. It is only the interpretation that differs.

If narrow lapels come in, a high-fashion interpretation might feature a puffed sleeve tapered at the wrist, while more traditional styling would employ a set-in sleeve that neither tapers nor flares. But make no mistake, major changes in style are reflected in both looks, although, of course, not as dramatically in the Classic Look.

High Fashion Chic ranges from fashion forward suits for business hours to avant garde sweatshirts for weekend wear. The Classic Look takes a more traditional approach. It's less trendy for work time, less daring for play time. Here are some outfitting examples of the two styles:

Before you make your choice between these two rich looks, consider your lifestyle and the type of clothing in which you'll feel comfortable, not outlandish. You can be wearing a one-of-a-kind design worth thousands, but if you think it's too flashy or too staid,

Above: *Classic business dress almost always features a hip-length jacket with an A-line skirt.*

Left: *High Fashion office wear tends to feature jackets that are longer or shorter, rarely in-between. When there is a notch-collar jacket, the vee tends to plunge deeper. Skirts at present are straighter and sparer.*

Left: *High Fashion casual wear tends to be sexier, more suggestive. Sweaters rarely have a collared shirt underneath. Pants taper at the ankle, are tighter in the rear.*

Right: *Classic casual wear features turtlenecks, fly-front, pleated slacks with straight legs, fuller cut.*

Evening outfits are demure, high-necked, long-sleeved in the Classic Look. Dresses usually fall right beneath the knee, and feature frills such as tucks and ruffles.

you'll feel uncomfortable and uncertain. It's that discomfort and uncertainty that will clearly give you away. Remember, a large part of looking rich is feeling right in what you're wearing.

We should also point out that you needn't decide to wear clothes that are exclusively High Fashion or Classic. Many women build a wardrobe that combines both styles of clothing. And some of the clothing itself isn't that easy to categorize. Giorgio Armani, for example, puts out a magnificent navy blue blazer with High Fashion features like narrow lapels and a double-breasted cut, yet its construction and tailoring are as Classic as a Brooks Brothers blazer.

You can also mix High Fashion and Classic garments and accessories in the same outfit. Not only is there nothing wrong with wearing an Oscar de la Renta blouse with something as simple and as basic as a Pendleton skirt, but many women find that by combining different fashion statements they create a look that is more personal, more their own.

One caution. High Fashion garments, by the very fact of being High Fashion, become dated much more quickly than more Classic clothes. And for the average-figured woman, they tend to be a little harder to wear. So unless you're independently wealthy and 5'10" and 118 pounds, perhaps it'd be a good idea to keep your basics, like suits and coats and slacks, on the Classic side, and do your accessorizing with more fashiony, highly styled items.

Opposite: *High Fashion evening wear tends to be a little more risqué, featuring lighter, lacier fabrics. Dresses will range from mini to maxi.*

2

"Packaging" Yourself

If you've ever wondered how one woman can look rich in a pair of five-pocket Western jeans, a chambray shirt, and a bandana around her neck, and another woman looks like she had to take out a loan to afford the Bill Blass original she is wearing, the answer is that it's all in the packaging. The cut of your hair, the shape and color of your nails, and the application of your makeup all make an important statement about you. If you don't trim your hair frequently enough in order to avoid the split and dead ends which make your hair dull and lifeless, and if you allow your nail polish to chip without giving your nails a quick patch-up job, it doesn't matter how expensive the Oscar de la Renta dress is. The total picture will be a tacky one.

Hair

There are several rich-looking hairstyles you can go with, but the key here is finding the one which best

Opposite: *The Chignon: the sleekest of Classic looks, pulled back from the face, high on the head or at the nape of the neck. It goes with every outfit on any occasion and can be worn by women of all ages.*

The Blunt Cut: distinctive in line and proportioned to the face and body, it can be worn all in one length, with or without bangs, or cut with a curl if you have a natural wave.

suits you. The photos in this chapter show the cuts you'd most likely see while brunching at New York's La Grenouille and dancing at Regine's: As Monsieur Marc, known for styling the hair of many very wealthy and elegant women, among them Nancy Reagan, confirms, "Your hair should be styled to your personality and be suited to you alone. A haircut is so much a part of a woman's image."

The most important things to consider when choosing your hairstyle are the proportion of hair length to your height and to your facial structure. "Every face

The Tousled Look: generally a layered cut. "It's the one in vogue among rich young women who prefer to be casual. They like looking undone. If they have naturally curly hair, they let it be curly," says Pierre Michel, another of Manhattan's posh coiffeurs. Worn slightly waved for business hours or curly and messy for wilder times, it's always rich looking. (This style fits more with the High Fashion look.)

Photography by Les Underhill for Pierre Michel.

Above: *The All-In-One-Length Cut: no longer a no-no for women who are past their 40s, this cut is simple, classically rich and best when worn at shoulder length, not longer.*

Opposite: *Tousled Short: cut longer in front and at the neck. Sides layered for fullness. Particularly good for those with finer features.*

Photography by Les Underhill for Pierre Michel.

Classic Short: a feathered, layered cut, longer on top, shorter at the sides. Classically feminine as each hair falls into place. Best when worn with a side part.

has to be studied individually. The hair must go with the face," says Nasser, of New York's chic Raymond and Nasser salon. For example, taller women are better able to carry off longer hairstyles than shorter women. On the other hand, shorter hair does work better on short women than it does on tall women. Women with narrow faces should wear hairstyles with fullness at the cheeks and chin while the opposite holds true for women with rounder faces.

Once you've picked the right hairstyle for you, make sure you get the proper cut. As Monsieur Marc comments, "Hair should be thought of as arranging a vase of flowers; one should work on it with an artistic feeling." So do place yourself in the hands of a skilled person, because skimping here may cost you your rich look!

Cut, condition and color are all-important. The richest looking hair is bouncy and natural at all times, styled freely and femininely rather than to an extreme. Elaborate "do's" are definitely don'ts.

Now that you have the cut, make sure you keep it in great condition. There's nothing in poorer taste than unkempt hair. Here are some tips from several top hairstylists whose clients are some of America's richest, chicest women:

1. Use a detangler after every shampooing.
2. Use a conditioner once a month, leaving it on the head for twenty minutes. Overdoing it will defeat your purpose as hair will turn limp and become difficult to style.
3. Trim your hair as frequently as needed. Putting this off will only make for more split ends and less rich-looking hair.

Coloring can be used as an option: it's best when used as a highlight. Do beware of your skin tone and choose a shade which complements your complexion. For example, Lord & Taylor's Glenn Conn suggests that women with ruddy complexions need ash tones to cool down the red in their skin, while those with olive complexions can choose warmer, red tones. Whatever you do, don't color to an extreme. It'll be time consuming, costly and tacky. The shades to avoid are: the purply-red that results from overdoing a henna treatment, the plastic white overbleached look, and multicolored highlighting which happens through excessive streaking. Excessive streaking can also make you look older when streaks appear as if they are gray, which occurs particularly under fluorescent lights.

Remember, the key to having rich-looking hair is to make sure it always looks like you've just had it done. Whether it's worn in a blunt cut or in a tousled style, every hair seems to be in place. The cut therefore is all-important. If you get a really good one, even after you wash it and blow-dry it, your hair will always fall perfectly.

Hands

Because your hands are so visible, caring for them is imperative. And it's caring that will add a great deal to the overall rich-looking you. If you're not as handy as you'd like to be, set aside the time to have a professional manicure once a week. The dollars will be well spent and in a short period of time there will be a significant improvement. It's a well-known fact that caring for your nails on a regular basis will get even the frailest of nails into shape. And, as long as you're having your fingernails done, treat yourself to a pedicure

Opposite: *Classic Long: layered at the sides for added fullness and softness. Feminine, tasteful, always in style . . . a fixture at Newport and debutante balls.*

once a month. Your feet will feel brand new. They'll look terrific. Let's face it, one key to looking rich is feeling rich.

The length of your nails should be in proportion to the size of your hands. However, classic nails tend to be a bit shorter than chic ones. Don't wear them too long, though, or you won't be able to function without breaking or chipping them. They'll become clawlike. Other definite don'ts are trendy colored polishes such as black or glittering metallics and appliques (no matter how small, they're tacky). Do:

1. Wear your nails all one length.
2. Make sure they are all shaped the same. Either they should be squared or rounded, never pointy.
3. Pick your nailpolish color to match your complexion and the colors in your wardrobe. The best bets are subtle reds, pinks and corals, wearing the lighter shades only if you have a tan or your skin tone is naturally dark.
4. Make sure your polish isn't chipped. If it happens, and it always does, touch it up on your own.
5. Make sure the polish on your toenails always matches the polish on your fingernails.

Once your hands are in shape, make sure they stay that way. If they really look great, one or two rings will emphasize them even more. But again, don't overdo it and load up your hands with rings on each finger. Remember, subtlety is the key to looking rich.

Skin

When rich skin comes to mind, you picture a flawless, silky complexion. Great skin takes discipline and commitment, but the rewards make it all worthwhile. If you can't afford to have cosmeticians working on your skin, there are several things you can do to make improvements or just maintain the healthy skin you do have. Follow these tips and make them part of your daily ritual:

1. Maintain a balanced diet, eliminating salt where possible.
2. Drink at least two to three eight-ounce glasses of water daily.
3. Get at least eight hours of sleep or try to catch a catnap or two during the day to make up for a late night.
4. Place a humidifier in the bedroom during the steam-heated winter months; try to cut down on summer air-conditioning.
5. Allow at least fifteen minutes in the morning and fifteen minutes at night for beauty care.

Things to remember:

1. Never apply cleansers and cremes with a Kleenex or towel. Instead, use your hands, making upward strokes on the face and circular movements on the forehead. Apply cleansers and cremes across the eyelids to the outside of the eyes and then toward the nose. Use lateral move-

ments on the throat and the back of your neck. When taking cleansers and cremes off, use a pad dipped in lukewarm water.

2. Use a lubricant around the eyes prior to cleansing in order to protect and shield the eye area from dryness.

3. Don't overdo a skin lubricant. "Like a plant, you can kill it by watering it too much," warns Georgette Klinger.

Products which may be of help:

1. Collagen Masques: these will nourish, firm and tighten dry and sensitive skin.

2. Moisturizing Masques: these are good as pick-ups when you're tired, great for puffiness around the eyes.

3. Cleansing Masques: used once a week, your skin will feel refreshed and healthy.

Before you use any product though, find out exactly what your skin type is. All you have to do is go to any major department store. You'll usually be able to get a free skin analysis.

Also test a product prior to using it by applying a dab of it on your wrist and seeing if you get a reaction within twenty-four hours. If not, it should be safe to use the product on your face.

Makeup

As in your clothing, moderation in your makeup is important for a rich and elegant look. You'll never see dark purple eyeshadow and overdone blush on a woman who's part of the horsey set at Fox Hills. Makeup should be used to enhance what you have, not make

The rich look in makeup means no hard lines, less makeup rather than more, soft muted eyeshadow (if you use any at all). Lipstick is fine, but only in the more natural tones and never with a harsh outline.

33

you look like a clown. "Eye makeup should complement the eye and not be too contrived," says Bert Feldman, skin specialist and beauty consultant at *i* Naturals, a chain of 147 cosmetic shops located throughout the U.S.

What's tacky:

1. Using too much rouge.
2. Not blending your rouge in well so you look as if you have blotches on your cheeks.
3. Using a foundation which doesn't match your skin tone. You'll get that line between your face and throat that looks awful and throws off your natural color.
4. Wearing eyeshadow that looks unnatural and contrived.

What's rich looking:

1. Using makeup gently and prettily. Younger women may be a bit more dramatic in their eye treatment but never harsh.
2. Blending makeup so there are no distinct lines on the face.
3. Having your lipstick color matching your nailpolish color.

Correcting common problems:

1. If your skin is too shiny, you may try using a foundation with less oil in it rather than using excessive amounts of powder.
2. If your cosmetics don't stay on long enough, use less moisturizer.

3. If you have a problem with your lipstick feathering, use a liplining pencil.

Keep in mind, cosmetics do lose their potency. So clean out your makeup case and get rid of what will do you no good. The average product life is twenty months.

If in doubt, it's always better to dress down than dress up; the same is true when it comes to makeup. If you're lucky enough to have terrific skin, you may be able to get away with no makeup at all. If not, use as little as possible, for subtlety is most important if you want that very rich look.

3

Shopping

Understanding quality and the importance of fit will make you a wiser and more successful shopper. In order to attain and maintain a rich look, you should get used to buying fewer pieces but better ones.

Quality

The trick of course is to get better for less. But be careful; make sure you give every garment a once over before you make your decision. Here's a checklist to follow so you don't run into any problems:

When you look at the fabric and tailoring

1. See if the lapels and collars have the proper interlinings and that the lapels are properly pressed (e.g., make sure there's no puckering). Less expensive clothing will have press-on interlinings which buckle and don't hold up under cleaning.
2. Look at the trimming, buttonholes and seams. There shouldn't be any loose threads sticking out. Seams should be double-stitched (so that the garment looks as if it were piped).
3. Check the quality of the seamtape on

hems and make sure that stitches don't show on the outside of those hems.

4. Stitching should be done neatly and evenly on garments, especially when the garments are patterned (e.g., plaids, stripes, checks). All seams should be perfectly matched, stripes to stripes, checks to checks.
5. Hemlines should be even, no peaks allowed.
6. Garments made in thin fabrics should hang straight. If they don't, and they are on their hangers correctly, the seams are puckering and the garment will be uneven on you.

Natural fabrics such as cotton, linen, silk, wool, cashmere, suede and leather are the ones with that extra rich appeal. These are the precious fabrics that say tasteful, well-made. However, there are natural and synthetic blends of excellent quality. But you should stick to those with higher natural fiber contents.

If you do go for the naturals, be especially aware of the care labels and for the imminent dry cleaning bills. When the label says hand wash, then do so by all means; but don't throw something with a "dry clean only" label into the washing machine or sink. Your rich look will be tacky in no time.

Natural fabrics are also known for wrinkling severely. Make sure you use your iron. While wrinkles are unavoidable and have been somewhat accepted, you'll never see Betsy Bloomingdale or the Princess of Wales looking like they've slept in their clothes for a week. Excessive wrinkling isn't chic, it's sloppy.

As far as synthetics are concerned, don't be afraid

they'll stand in your way to a rich look. When blended with the naturals, price may come down but there's no let up in quality. Also, silk and crepe de Chine imitations of 100 percent polyester are terrific. Jack Mulqueen's "silksational" is among the very best and no one will ever know the difference.

Fit

The importance of the proper fit can't be stressed enough. The most exquisite and expensive of Yves St. Laurent designs won't make you look rich if it doesn't fit. Buy the right size for you, not the size you'd like to wear. And understand, your size will vary, as different manufacturers use different specifications. For example, when you're out shopping one day, you may fit into a size 8 in a pair of Harvé Benard trousers and also fit into a size 10 in the same style pant by Calvin Klein.

When it comes to fit, the two most common mistakes made by women are wearing things too tight and too loose. While the subtlely oversized look is very rich in high fashion circles, the lost-in look seems more impoverished than wealthy. On the other hand, the poured-in look is more vampy than classy. Remember,

Opposite: *Note how the pattern lines up perfectly on Calvin Klein's handsome wool plaid dress—the sure sign of a well-made piece of clothing. When a woman walks into a room and you suddenly find yourself thinking,* Gee, she looks rich, *it's dozens of little details like this that are leading you to such a conclusion. A poorly matching pattern gives an opposite message.*

anything taken to an extreme works to your disadvantage; rich becomes tacky.

Make sure you avoid: collars that stand away; sleeves that are too long; hemlines that are too short or too long for your height (e.g., a midcalf skirt shortens a short woman). Even though designers say mini to maxi lengths are right, the proportions of your body and a glance in the mirror will tell you what length is right for you.

4

Clothing

Developing your rich-looking wardrobe is the next step. The most common misconception is that you can never wear the same thing twice and look rich. Well, wearing the same skirt or pair of trousers in the same week isn't wrong at all; it's encouraged. In fact, the key is:

— limiting the number of pieces in your wardrobe
— concentrating on separates that mix and match
— mixing and matching expensive with inexpensive
— using accessories to add excitement
— establishing a palette of neutral colors to serve as a springboard, and using some bold-colored extras to serve as accents

Here's how to do it. Pick out two or three neutral colors, making sure that the colors work well with your complexion. Navy and taupe will best fit into the classic scheme of things as will black and gray for high fashion. White works for both, and the barriers of only after Easter and before Labor Day no longer exist. Using these colors as your core for suits, separate jackets, skirts and pants, you'll be able to use colorful

solid and patterned blouses, shirts and sweaters as accent pieces. Colors which have a richness to them are deep reds and purples, tapestry hues such as jade and teal, and the brights such as fuchsia and cobalt blue. With the right accessories and finishing touches, you'll find your base palette can be elegant when you want it to be and as ready as you wish.

While the number of items you purchase will depend upon your particular budget, the core of your wardrobe should consist of two to three suits (with different style jackets and skirts), two or three pairs of well-fitting trousers/pants, one cashmere sweater, one trenchcoat and one super winter coat. With these, mixing and matching will become easy. For example, you may wear one suit on a Monday. On Tuesday, you could wear the suit jacket with a pair of trousers. The next day you may decide on the skirt and cashmere sweater and so on and so forth. As you can see:

Before we start outfitting, here's a guideline to the richest fabrics and styling details for High Fashion and Classic Looks. Remember, these are guidelines and looks to go after, so if you can't afford a suede shirt, you can opt for the same surface interest by buying a great brushed flannel top.

Opposite: *The cap-sleeved, patterned silk blouse with contrasting silk trousers, tapered at the ankle.*

Left: *The silk patterned blouse and shirt with solid silk double-breasted jacket.*

Right: *The silk double-breasted jacket with contrasting silk trousers, tapered at the ankle.*

Opposite: *The patterned silk skirt worn with an angora cardigan (note pearl beading), buttoned up the back.*

This one blouse has it all yet remains understated. Note the asymmetrical closing, dropped shoulder, French cuffs and blouson look in this silk, high fashion blouse.

BLOUSES:

	HIGH FASHION	*CLASSIC*
Fabrics:	silk	cotton oxford
	crepe de Chine	silk
	cotton	flannel
	linen	denim
	suede	
	leather	
	denim	
	taffeta	
	tissue faille	
	challis	
Styling:	dropped shoulders	fitted
	looseness under armholes and at the waistline when tucked in or worn out and belted	button-down collar
		regular cuff
		Peter Pan collar
	raglan sleeves	
	French cuff	
	tucked front	
	asymmetrical neckline	

VESTS:

	HIGH FASHION	*CLASSIC*
Fabrics:	leather	wool
	suede	cashmere
	silk	denim
	cashmere	corduroy
Styling:	blousy	fitted
	button front	pullover
	V neck	V neck
		crew neck

Above: *Note the Peter Pan collar, fitted bodice and cuff of one of the most classic shirting looks in cotton oxford. A ribbon placed under the collar and tied in front and a bow tie are rich-looking approaches.*

Opposite: *The vest, while rarely expensive, creates a unique look and can add variety to a substantial number of outfits within your wardrobe. Here's a classic wool vest trimmed in velvet. It's shown with a crisp cotton bow-tied blouse and cuffed trousers.*

SKIRTS:

	HIGH FASHION	CLASSIC
Fabrics:	gabardine	gabardine
	wool challis	wool challis
	silk broadcloth	cotton
	wool	poplin
	silk	wool
	linen	denim
	suede	seersucker
	leather	
	denim	
Styling:	straight	A-lined
	dropped waistline	wrap
	dirndl	full-circle
	divided	pleated
	slits (back, front or side)	culottes

SWEATERS:

	HIGH FASHION	CLASSIC
Fabrics:	wool	wool
	cashmere	cashmere
	cotton	cotton
Styling:	oversized jacketlike (e.g.: wrap, shawl-collared)	fitted
	drop-shouldered	crew neck
	turtleneck	V neck
	crew neck	cardigan
	bateau	turtleneck

50

Left: *Note the straight, spare shape on this high fashion skirt with back slit.*

Right: *Note the fuller cut of the classic skirt, worn just below the knee.*

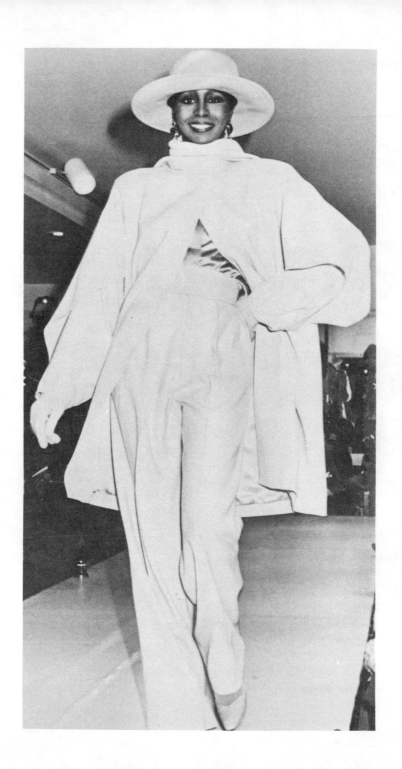

PANTS:

	HIGH FASHION	CLASSIC
Fabrics:	wool	wool
	gabardine	gabardine
	silk	poplin
	linen	seersucker
	suede	cotton
	leather	
	denim	
	silk broadcloth	
	wool challis	
Styling:	fly-front pleated trouser	fly-front pleated trouser
	clean front pant	pleatless pant
	side-zipped	jeans
	back-zipped	cuffs
	dropped waistline	straight-legged
	tapered to the ankle	
	wide-legged	
	jeans	

Opposite: *High fashion, pleated-front trousers, from Albert Nipon.*

Left: *The classic clean front, pleatless pant with straight leg.*

Center: *These pleated, side-zipped walking shorts fit into both the Classic and High Fashion looks. Treated classically here, the shorts are teamed with a high-necked, tucked-front cotton blouse and Shetland crew-neck sweater thrown over the shoulders.*

Right: *These shorts can go High Fashion or Classic. Shown here with the classic polo shirt but high fashion socks and tasseled slip-in flats.*

The wide-notched lapel and drop-shouldered details add elegance to this two-piece dress from Calvin Klein. The rolled-up sleeves are another rich effect. It is the kind of outfit that can spark an existing wardrobe and be worn forever.

SHORTS:

	HIGH FASHION	*CLASSIC*
Fabrics:	wool	wool
	gabardine	gabardine
	silk	poplin
	linen	seersucker
	suede	cotton
	leather	
	denim	
Styling:	walking	walking
	running	running
		Bermuda
		cuffed

DRESSES:

	HIGH FASHION	*CLASSIC*
Fabrics:	silk	silk
	crepe de Chine	cashmere
	linen	wool challis
	cashmere	cotton
	angora	
	cotton	
	wool challis	
	suede	
	leather	
	wool jersey	
Styling:	chemise	shirtwaist
	dropped waistline	A-lined
	tucked-front	tucked-front
	asymmetrical	wrap
	dimple-sleeved	

The classic shirtdress in silk.

JACKETS:

	HIGH FASHION	CLASSIC
Fabrics:	wool	wool
	suede	suede
	leather	sable
	silver fox	chinchilla
	red fox	corduroy
	opossum	
Styling:	bomber	traditional blazer
	¾ coat	wrap
	pleated sleeve	set-in shoulder
	raglan sleeve	pea coat
	double-breasted	single-breasted

COATS:

	HIGH FASHION	CLASSIC
Fabrics:	cashmere	cashmere
	wool	wool
	leather	sable
	suede	chinchilla
	corduroy	mohair
	silver fox	
	red fox	
	opossum	

Opposite: *Ruffled lapel shapes this high fashion short wool crepe jacket from Albert Nipon. Outfit is completed with straight mock-wrap skirt and solid charmeuse blouse adorned with cowl tie neckline. Both skirt and jacket can be mixed and matched to create literally dozens of other outfits.*

Above: *The blazer can be worn for business with a patterned or solid full skirt or for leisure with jeans. The pleated sleeve and slightly padded shoulders update this classic jacket.*

Opposite: *High fashion suede with shoulder pads to accentuate the dropped-shoulder detail.*

COATS
(con't)

Styling:

wrap	tailored
⅞'s length	double-breasted
notch-collared	princess
shawl-collared	trenchcoat
raglan sleeve	
caped trenchcoat	
ponchos	
dropped shoulder	

SWIMSUITS:

	HIGH FASHION	*CLASSIC*
Fabrics:	Lycra Spandex	Lycra Spandex
Styling:	maillot	maillot
	thong	
	bikini	
	high-cut leg	

Opposite: *Whether your style is High Fashion or Classic, having a trenchcoat in your wardrobe is a must. This Burberry raincoat is truly one of the richest and most classic of looks. Great for business and weekends.*

The thong, a favorite on the beaches in St. Tropez, is a high-fashion version of the one-piece suit.

The classic maillot, either solid or patterned, can be seen on the beaches at Newport and Southampton. It's a sexy look, yet only the shoulders, arms and legs are bared. Matching cover-ups and sweatsuits add to the richness of the total look. Note: a higher cut on the leg will make your legs appear to be longer and thinner.

5

Mixing and Matching

In the preceding chapters we've pointed out specific items of clothing that suggest that the woman who is wearing them has both money and style. Here we're going to concentrate on how you can mix and match rich-looking garments to create an overall look, one that instantly identifies you as someone with a superior sense of sophistication and taste.

The outfits shown in this chapter are a blending of garments characterized by clean lines and few frills. Note the subtlety in jewelry and accessories that enhances rather than overwhelms.

Fourteen Smashing Effects

One of the least expensive, and often most dramatic, ways to create a rich-looking outfit is to juxtapose a costly item with something as ordinary as a pair of Levi's. For example, mix a pair of Gucci loafers with a pair of nineteen dollar L. L. Bean khakis; match a Calvin Klein cashmere coat with a ninety dollar Liz Claiborne sweater dress.

Here are fourteen more smashing effects with

High Fashion
Left: *Crepe de Chine tucked-front chemise with padded shoulders, contrast collar and cuffs worn here with the menswear-shaped bow tie for the high fashion look.*

Classic
Right: *The classic look's version of the dropped waistline wool crepe dress with full sleeves and skirt.*

High Fashion
Left: *High fashion's pleated sleeve and padded shoulders on the shirttailed-bottom T dress in a cotton knit. The accessories make a big difference.*

Classic
Right: *Classic knit shirtdress. Note the tee-shirt collar, full, knee length skirt. Very simple. Very rich-looking.*

Classic
Roll-tab sleeved, patched-pocket silk blouse. Basic, classic,
chic. Works well with suits and separate skirts, trousers
and walking shorts.

which you can create a rich look as simply as changing your belt:

—Slip on a snakeskin belt with a pair of jeans.
—Wear a pearl choker with an open-necked oxford shirt and V neck pullover sweater.
—Turn up the collar of a polo shirt and put on some pearl earrings.
—Wear a scarf tied as an ascot with an open-collared silk blouse.
—Tie a silk scarf to the handle or strap of your handbag.
—Stick a stickpin on the lapel of your blazer or jacket.
—When wearing an ordinary outfit to an ordinary place, carry an extraordinary

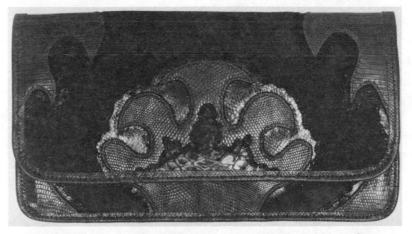

Carlos Falchi reptile skin bag. More High Fashion than Classic, which makes it fun and intriguing to wear with Lily Pulitzer shift. Not inexpensive, but a purchase that will last and add elegance forever.

handbag like a Carlos Falchi or a Bottega Veneta. The latter is distinguished by a weave so unique, that although the bag sports no designer initials or well-known logo, others will recognize it in an instant.

—Wear opaque tights or sheer stockings in colors to match your outfits.

—Wear diamond studs with jeans and an oxford shirt.

—Wear pearls with sweatsuits.

—Put on a terrific watch; make sure bands may be interchanged so you can match your outfits.

—Dress up your bathing suit with a gold chain or bangle.

—Wear sunglasses with a unique frame, such as leather.

—Throw a sweater over your shoulders and tie sleeves in front.

Nine Rich Outfits for about $150

Putting together a rich outfit for approximately $150.00 is easier than you think. Here are nine of them. When thrown together correctly, they look absolutely sensational . . . much more expensive than their actual cost.

Opposite: *The Angora top with a sweater worn over the shoulders and tied in front.*

Casual

1. A white Izod polo shirt with turned-up collar worn with a Levi's denim skirt and an A. Peter Pushbottom red cotton knit sweater thrown over the shoulders. Add white opaque tights and Topsiders.
2. A Merona pink and white striped rugby shirt worn with Merona pink pull-on, straight-legged pants piped in white, white crocheted anklets, and a pair of pink Keds.
3. A Pendleton red and grey striped cardigan, and grey cotton pleated trousers with grey ribbed knee-highs and tasseled loafers.

Business

1. A Liz Claiborne Angora V-necked, ¾ sleeve sweater dress with matching sheer stockings and leather pumps.
2. Clyde's navy box-pleated wool skirt with a button-down collared white oxford shirt and navy/burgundy/white patterned bow tie. Use navy tights and spectacular pumps.
3. A Ralph Lauren polo tee-shirt dress accessorized with a great webbed belt, tights and matching flats.

Evening

1. A Jack Mulqueen black and white striped silk shirt dress, black sheer stockings and black patent leather, open-toe, slingback heels.

Opposite: *The full raglan-sleeved, diagonally striped dress emphatically belted at the waist.*

Classic
Above: *The puffed sleeve peasant blouse in cotton batiste.*
Wear it worn off one shoulder for a look that's très risqué.

High Fashion
Opposite: *The low Veed, padded shoulder, one-button*
braid-trimmed wool crepe jacket with matching dirndl
skirt. The high-necked blouse shown here works well for
business and for an evening out.

2. A white A. Peter Pushbottom crew-neck cable cotton knitted sweater worn belted out over Finity white linen walking shorts, white sheer stockings, and white patent tuxedo flats.

3. Ellen Tracy black faille pants worn with a Leon Max white tucked-front cotton tuxedo shirt, black silk cummerbund and bow tie, black sheer stockings and black-bowed tuxedo flats.

Ten Outfits from One Suit

Here's what a little mixing and matching can do. Begin with a three-piece suit in a basic color. For example, take a Harvé Benard notch-collared and double-breasted jacket, dirndl skirt, and pleated, cuffed trousers. Add one cream-colored, silk-ruffled, high-neck blouse and a pale pink cashmere cardigan sweater. Wear them in these combinations:

1. Jacket, skirt
2. Jacket, skirt, silk blouse
3. Skirt, silk blouse, cardigan
4. Skirt, silk blouse
5. Skirt, cardigan (buttons to the back this time)
6. Jacket, trousers, silk blouse
7. Trousers, silk blouse, cardigan sweater thrown over the shoulders, tied in front

Classic
Opposite: *The classic gabardine blazer with matching pleated A-line skirt, worn here with a striped oxford shirt and ribbon tie. A change to a silk-bowed blouse at the end of the work day prepares you for an evening at the theatre.*

8. Trousers, silk blouse worn out and belted
9. Trousers, cardigan
10. Jacket, trousers, cardigan (button to the back)

These are just a few of the looks you can create by mixing and matching. Once the basic pieces are there, putting great combinations together is both easy and fun.

6

Recycling and Creating

Some of the richest-looking outfits you most admire are the result of either recycling old clothes or literally starting them from scratch. Tailors can work miracles on clothes you never thought you'd wear again; and if you have the time to sew, you can make your own rich clothes by choosing the right styles for you among the many designer patterns available.

Recycling

Take a look through your closet and you're sure to find clothes that've just been hanging there because they're not "in fashion" and you haven't had the heart to throw them out. Well, you don't have to throw them out. In fact, a few alterations and they'll seem new.
Some suggestions are:

—Have wide lapels on jackets made narrower.
—Have collars that are too long made shorter.
—Make dresses that've gotten too short into blouses.

—Taper wide-legged pants.

—Make wide-legged pants into culottes or walking shorts.

—Have the bottoms of wide-legged pants tapered to the ankle.

—Change the buttons on an old blazer or jacket and have it relined.

—Shorten formal dresses into great shorter ones.

—Have waistbands taken in or let out.

The charges for alterations such as these vary among tailors but you should be able to get buttons changed for no more than two dollars and lapels narrowed on winter coats at no more than forty-five dollars. The prices for the other changes mentioned fall somewhere in between, ranging from five dollars to fifteen dollars for pants, skirts and shirts and from twenty dollars to thirty dollars for dresses. Any way you look at it, you'll have a new piece in your wardrobe for considerably less.

Creating

If you have the time and the talent for sewing, you've got it made. Designer patterns are now available through catalogs such as Vogue, Simplicity and McCalls. Ranging in price from $4.50 to $9.50 for

High Fashion
Opposite: *Crepe de Chine skirt worn just at the knee with matching tulip-bodiced blouse which has padded shoulders and pleated sleeves for a high fashion look.*

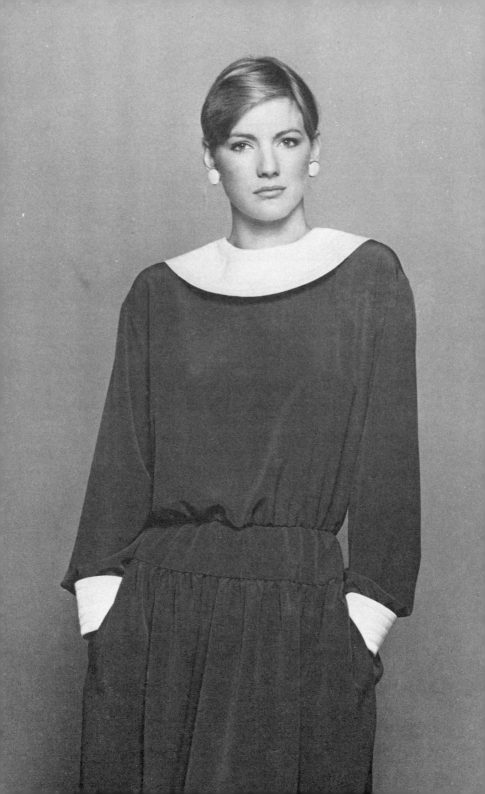

High Fashion
Above: *Tweed asymmetric oversized jacket with leather pants, full on top, tapered at the ankle.*

Classic
Opposite: *Demure silk dress with white rounded shoulder yoke and cuffs in the classic style.*

dress, sportswear and even bridal gown patterns by American, French and Italian designers such as Calvin Klein, Perry Ellis, Ralph Lauren, Valentino and Chloe, the only other things you need are the fabric and sewing machine. You'll find the measurements for sizing and what you'll need in terms of notions and fabric beside the illustrations in the pattern book. If you're a knitter or want to take the time to learn, you can make some wonderful designer sweaters as well.

"I buy expensive fabrics that may cost thirty dollars to fifty dollars a yard (they're generally sixty-four inches wide) so while the outfit may end up costing me $250, I would have had to pay perhaps $1200 at retail for it," says Sunny Griffin, the television talk show hostess. Griffin stresses the importance of buying fine fabrics and makes use of the discount fabric houses such as Poli on New York's chic Fifty-seventh Street. She recommends:

—buying what you need all at one time because the fabric you are working with may not be there later that same day.
—working with heavy wools as they are the easiest, and never buying the sleazy lightweight wools.
—staying away from soft satiny-finished fabrics, such as silk charmeuse, as they are extremely difficult to work with.

High Fashion
Opposite: *Suede raglan-sleeved jacket worn with a cowl neck sweater and cropped pants. The belt and boots are important accessories here.*

Make sure you know what size you need. Pattern sizes are standardized by the government and may vary from the clothes you have been buying from particular manufacturers. "I normally wear a size 10 but I take a size 12 in patterns," adds Sunny.

Also it is obviously best if you learn to sew well. "I find my Swiss Berneia machine is best. It has a knee lift that frees both your hands. I also recommend buying lots of attachments; they'll enable you to do some fine detailing such as scallops and appliqués," says Sunny.

7

Accessorizing

Accessories such as belts, scarves and jewelry can and do make or break the richest looking of outfits. You can dress up, dress down, make trendy, or make classic any piece in your wardrobe by using the right accessories. For example, take your basic black cotton jersey tee-shirt dress. A classic approach for accessorizing would be to dress it up with only a strand of pearls, pearl earrings and a Cartier watch, or dress it down with a Coach leather belt, pearl earrings and a sweater thrown over the shoulders. A more High Fashion approach is to add a white leather cummerbund, a white linen jacket, gold necklace, earrings and bracelet for a night out, and a low-slung concha belt (to give the dress a blousoned look) and some wooden or geometric jewelry for a more casual occasion.

Belts

The richest of looks in belts are listed below. High fashion belts tend to be more elaborate, and classic, less ornate.

Best for daytime:

constructed	narrow
double wrap	sculptured buckles
high-hip slouch	studded

silver/gold	concha
reptile	suede
cabachon stoned	leather

Best for night:

deco	jet
suede	faceted stoned
rhinestone	cummerbunds

Jewelry

Whether you opt for the real thing or choose the imitations, jewelry is a must for looking rich. The essentials on your list should be:

—a strand of pearls
—a gold chain
—a pair of pearl earrings
—a pair of diamond studs
—a pair of gold dots
—a gold bangle bracelet
—a gold watch which allows you to interchange bands
—beads

All the above are on the must-have lists of both High Fashion and Classic dressers; however, the settings of the individual pieces may differ. For example, a Classic look would be a simple gold necklace or several gold chains of the same length twisted (most commonly seen with beads, called forsade) to appear as one, while a Chic approach would be a sculptured gold necklace or a necklace of three colors of gold (yellow, rose and white) interlocked.

Pearls, because they go with everything, are a focal

point for your jewelry wardrobe. There are several styles from which you can choose.

Styles of Pearls

Choker: a uniform pearl necklace that drops just above the collarbone

Princess: eighteen inches in length

Matinee: twenty inches to twenty-four inches in length

Opera: twenty-eight inches to thirty inches in length

Bib: a pearl necklace of more than three strands

Rope: a necklace forty-five inches or more in length (also called sautoir or lariot)

The Princess, Matinee and Opera lengths are more in the old money classic style, while all six of the above styles would fit into the high fashion wardrobe.

If you decide to invest in a strand of real pearls, there are a number of things you should know.

1. Lustre. Lustre depends upon the reflection of light from the surface of the pearl. Generally, the more coatings, the deeper and more brilliant the lustre.

2. Orient. Orient is the result of refraction of light through the various layers of nacre. It enhances the lustre of the pearl and gives it a unique quality.

3. Cleanliness. This refers to absence of blemishes; the fewer of them, the higher the value of the pearl.

4. Color. Pearls come in an almost infinite variety of hues and shades ranging from pink to gold through green, blue, silver and black, but the most important color for any woman is the one that flatters her the most. Rose tones complement a fair complexion and

darker shades are best for creamy or white skins.

5. Size. The size of a pearl is measured by its diameter in millimeters (a millimeter is approximately 1/25th of an inch). Generally, prices increase as the size increases due to the fact that larger pearls are scarce. However, size is only one factor in determining the quality and value of a pearl.

6. Shape. Pearls are in many shapes. Round is perfectly spherical while baroque is irregular. There are also pear, drop, button and inobe (half-round).

7. Matching. No two pearls are ever exactly alike. Most necklaces are the result of a careful blending of pearls which appear to look alike in respect to color, lustre and size.

Once you make your purchase, remember, pearls should be taken care of. Keep them free from dirt, perfume, cosmetics and perspiration. Wipe pearls frequently with a damp cloth and have them restrung at least once a year. They should not be worn on hands or wrists which will be exposed to laundry detergents or when bathing.

Earrings are easy to forget about, but shouldn't be. They are essential in creating a rich look, and are often all that is needed to transform a merely pleasant outfit into one that makes a formidable statement.

Among the more classic styles are the button, for office hours; the hoop, for more casual times; and the drop, for dressier occasions. When choosing earrings, consider the shape of your face. For example, a square or broad face would not look good with a large domed type of earring. That makes the face appear even broader. According to Monet's fashion coordinator, Charlotte Left, a person with this shaped face would be better off with a hoop, drop or flat-type button style. Left goes on to point out, "If one has a short neck, drop earrings are generally not good. A plumper face needs to give an illusion of length by wearing elongated shapes. A thin or long face can wear a variety of styles but must be careful not to wear drops or hoops that are too long." While Classic dressers would stay with gold, silver, pearls, diamonds, and other precious stones such as sapphire, High Fashion women may opt to add earrings of materials such as leather (which has been referred to as the "new gold" in fashion circles), wood and Lucite.

Beads, for the High Fashion types, can make an important fashion statement. Many younger women are wearing them. They come in wood, Lucite, and perhaps the most popular are those of glass, which are available in several colors. Twisting four, ten or twelve strands together, called forsade, can make for a very rich look. Also, somewhere in between fine and costume jewelry are such things as ivory, jade, amber and garnet beads. Semiprecious stones such as amethyst, black onyx and lapis are popular as well. According to Fernanda Gilligan, in public relations at Cartier, "Sapphires are particularly popular and the use of colored stones and semiprecious stones together in necklaces and bracelets is being seen more." If you are in the market for something a little bit different, you may want to look at some irregularly shaped semiprecious stones called tumbled beads. They sell for about twenty-two dollars a strand, are available in many different colors and can be very rich looking when worn with the appropriate clothing.

When you are picking out the jewelry for a particular outfit, remember to think about the style, shape and design of the pieces. If they are fabulous looking yet don't belong with the outfit you are wearing, your rich look will go down the drain. Also, keep in mind that overdoing it will kill your rich look as well. "Women tend to wear too much jewelry. They should wear two to three items, not five or six. They should buy quality, not quantity. They should consider the neckline of the outfit, the fabric and the style in selecting jewelry," says Harry Winston's Norma Smith. For example, the heavier the fabric, the chunkier the jewelry can be; the lighter the outfit, the more delicate the jewelry. You wouldn't want to be caught dead in a frilly little sundress with clunky wooden beads.

Scarves can be the extra added touch that completes many rich-looking outfits. With a little practice, you can get the basic knots down pat and use your imagination for more intricate styling. For example, use the small square for the gaucho or bandana look, the large square for the flip knot and ruffle, and the oblong for the ascot and slip knot.

As you can see, the options are many. While accessorizing is a must to complete an outfit, keep in mind it should never be overdone.

Here a high fashion blouse is mixed with a traditionally styled skirt. A concha belt is the go-between, giving the outfit a dramatically richer look than it would have unbelted.

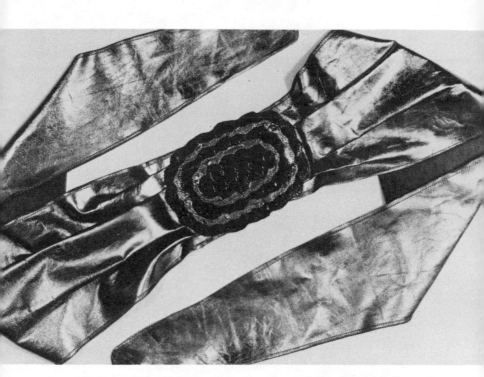

*High fashion satin leather wrap from Carlos Falchi. Imag-
ine how it could dress up "The Little Black Dress."*

*A modern version of a classic pants suit is given flair,
shape and a whole lot more interest by the addition of a belt.*

*Diamond studs are appropriate for either a High Fashion
or Classic look. If you can't afford the real thing, consider
zircons. Only your jeweler will know for sure. Whether
you're headed out for dinner at the best restaurant in town,
or racing through the supermarket in a sweatshirt and
jeans, it's little touches like the above that connote style,
money, charisma.*

The rich look in jewelry is less rather than more. "Women tend to wear too much jewelry. They should wear two to three items, not five or six," says Norma Smith of Harry Winston

Rich-looking Blassport scarf is stylishly knotted to the side, full not skimpy, the same material and pattern as the outfit it adorns.

Sometimes the most obviously inexpensive piece of costume jewelry like these single beads gives you a rich look because it says, I don't give a damn. I'm wearing this for me.

8

Shoe-ing

As in buying clothing, understated is the best way to go when you're looking for shoes. You'll find if you stick to neutral colors and basic shapes, a few pairs can go a long way.

The must haves:

—Three pairs of basic pumps; black, navy and taupe are your best bets and they go with everything. Closed toes and backs are the most practical but one pair of open toes and a pair of slingbacks (such as one classic favorite, the Chanel shoe) are fine.

—One pair of terrific boots either flat or low heeled. Avoid those spike-heeled leather suede boots.

—Two or three pairs of casual shoes; flats are best. Those with a classic style will prefer penny loafers and Topsiders while the high fashion woman will go for the more updated flats with details such as whipstitching and interweaving.

—One pair of evening pumps or sandals, best in black satin.

—If you have some leftover money in your shoe budget after you've bought your "must haves," go ahead and treat yourself to those shoes you've had your eye on but only go with one or two of your outfits.

Below are some examples of the richest-looking shoes for Classic and High Fashion wardrobes:

The casual leather flat.

The basic leather pump.

When you're buying your shoes, remember to buy shoes that fit well. No matter how beautiful the shoe is, if it's a little too tight or a little too loose it will throw off your walk. Since how you carry yourself is a major factor in how you appear to others, this little detail can throw off your rich look as well. Remember, too, that once you make your purchase, keep your shoes looking as if they were always brand new. Keep

The low-heeled suede and leather boot.

them polished if they are leather and brushed if they are suede. When you find your lifts (on the bottom of the heels) wearing down, go straight to the shoemaker and have new ones put on. There is almost nothing tackier than walking around in shoes whose heels look like they've been on a forced march or two.

It may seem a small detail, but the right shoes enhance the look you've put together in your clothing. Stick to basics that go from morning till night and you'll see a closet full of shoes isn't a necessity for looking rich.

9

Finishing Touches

The finishing touches such as handbags, hats, gloves, pantyhose/stockings and perfumes are what complete your total rich-looking picture.

Handbags

It's important to have a great handbag because of its visibility. You no longer have to worry about having a handbag match the color of an outfit; just go for a leather or suede bag (in a neutral color) of quality for daytime. Shoulder bags are the most practical for business and look less awkward when you're carrying a briefcase or envelopes. High fashion chic wears this bag for casual times as well, old money classic may opt for the ever popular Bermuda bag.

For evening, small clutch or shoulder bags in fabrics such as moire, satin, velvet and deco beading are outfit makers. Petit point bags are old money classic favorites.

Hats

They have become a revived fashion focal point. Fedoras (with narrow and wide brims) are best for high

Black leather gloves only enhance the elegance of a suit, the richness of the overall look.

Courtesy of Bill Blass

fashion chic while berets and picture hats fit better in the old money classic wardrobe.

Gloves

A minor detail yet not one to be overlooked. You won't see rich-looking mittens unless you are skiing at Vail, Colorado or ice skating at New York's Rockefeller Center, so avoid wearing them unless you too are sporting. Suede, leather and pigskin gloves are among the richest looking and work for day and evening. Wrist length or higher is fine when warmth is a factor. Elbow length is a bit dramatic when warmth is not a factor and should be avoided.

Pantyhose/Stockings

Dressing the leg is another outfit completer. Listed below are the most important looks. Those who prefer classic styling should select the natural sheers, the more subtle shades in pantyhose/stockings. High fashion dresses can use both subtle and bold colors in sheers and opaques, the latter more as accent pieces, employing the pantyhose as an accessory.

Sheers and opaques in pastels and rich colors for day, lace effects and shines for evening.

Leg Warmers

One of fashion's practical novelties. Works for both the High Fashion and Classic styles in ribs, jacquards, crochets. Can be layered but avoid making your calves look too big and out of proportion.

Socks

Ankle, crew and knee-highs work in argyles, plaids, tweeds and solids. Luxury fabrics, such as cashmere, crochets, ribs and herringbones are among the richest.

Make sure:

1. You never have a run in your pantyhose/stockings.

2. You don't wear open shoes if your pantyhose/stockings have a reinforced toe or heel; it's very tacky.

3. Your leg warmers and socks match what you are wearing. For example, argyle socks won't go with polka dot walking shorts.

Perfumes

A rich scent isn't really a matter of money. It is the ingredients in the particular perfume and how they react with your skin that ultimately says luxury. Jasmine and roses have an elegant and rich air on some, while the heavier, more pungent Oriental perfumes work better for others.

When testing a new fragrance, you should sample one at a time and see how they react on you. If you are testing fragrances in a store, don't try any more than three different ones at one time because they'll all begin to smell alike. Put a drop at your wrists and also at the bend of your elbows. According to Annette Green, the director of the Fragrance Foundation, "The aroma should be noticed within a twelve-inch circle around you."

Fragrance application is very similar to that of cosmetics. For example, if your skin is dry, you'll need to use more of a certain fragrance and you will have to apply it more frequently than those with oily skin. If you perspire heavily, you'll need to wear a lighter fragrance. The three steps in applying your fragrance should be:

—using toilet water and splashing it over your body.

—using perfume at the pulse points such as wrists, elbows, ankles and neck.

—using cologne, as it is the lightest form of fragrance, to refresh during the day.

All three should of course be in the same fragrance.

Different fragrances do say different things about you, so you may want to use one for business, one for sporting and one for evening. Again, it is a fact that a major factor in looking rich is feeling rich.

If you'd love to lavish yourself in the richest of fragrances but don't think you have the budget to do so, you may want to opt for the generic versions of the most popular perfumes. Jean Richelle Parfums, Ltd. specializes in the replicas of originals such as Opium, Bal a Versailles, Chanel #5, Chloe, Halston, Joy, Oscar de la Renta, L'air du Temps, Shalimar and Youth Dew. Available in Parfum for $9.50 per ½ ounce (as opposed to Opium @ $130.00 per ounce) and Eau de Toilette for $8.50 for two ounces, you may purchase your favorite fragrance by mail order. Write to Jean

Richelle Parfums, Ltd., whose address is listed in the Appendix, p. 00. No one will know the difference and you will smell and feel like you're worth a million.

Once the finishing touches are added, your rich look is complete. Whether it is High Fashion or Classic Rich you're after, these look completers do make a difference.

Addendum

Now that you know what to buy, you're probably wondering where to buy it all without spending a fortune. Below, we've listed over ninety of the best stores in the United States to find High Fashion and Classic clothing at reasonable prices. All the stores chosen carry garments of the highest quality; many even offer discounts from regular retail prices.

A. Peter Pushbottom
1157 Second Avenue
New York, N.Y.
(212) 759-1336
Major Credit Cards
Wide range of colors in cotton knit sweaters and Classic styles.

Annie Sez
Rt. 46 East
Clifton, N.J.
(201) 772-2211
Major Credit Cards
Other locations: Shrewsbury, Bloomfield, Montvale, Paramus, Millburn, Greenbrook, N.J.; Hartsdale, N.Y.
Domestic and imported designer clothing. 25%–60% off regular retail. High Fashion and Classic styles.

Arrival Fashions
150 Orchard Street
New York, N.Y.
(212) 673-8992
Major Credit Cards
Great discounts, large selection for High Fashion and
Classic looks.

Azriel Altman
204 Fifth Avenue
New York, N.Y.
(212) 889-0782
Domestic and French imports at 30%–50% discounts.
Great selection. Generally Classic, but some High
Fashion.

Bandwagon
1176 Hamburg Turnpike
Wayne, N.J.
(201) 696-5000
Major Credit Cards
Moderate/Better designer merchandise. 30%–70% off
regular retail. High Fashion and Classic styles.

Bank's
615 First Avenue
Minneapolis, Minn.
(612) 379-2810
Brand-name clothing, shoes, accessories at 50% off
regular retail. High Fashion and Classic.

Benetton
601 Madison Avenue
New York, N.Y.
(212) 751-3155
Major Credit Cards
Great for knits. Classic styles.

Bolton's
225 East 57th Street
New York, N.Y.
(212) 755-2527
Major Credit Cards
Other locations: White Plains, New Rochelle, Cedar-
hurst, N.Y.; Paramus, N.J.
Sportswear and everything else. Good selection at
20%–50% off regular retail prices. High Fashion and
Classic looks.

The Best Things
77 Delancey Street
New York, N.Y.
(212) 925-8395
Major Credit Cards
Clothes for the working woman. Classic styles. 20%–
50% discounts.

Conn-Co.
7820 Olson Memorial St. Hwy. 55
Golden Valley, Minn.
(612) 544-0766
Other locations: 11 stores in the Twin Cities, Fargo,
Sioux Falls.
Name-brand clothes at 20%–40% discounts. Mostly
casual sportswear. Young looks. Classic.

Cazou
1365 Sixth Avenue
New York, N.Y.
(212) 246-2666
Other locations: Philadelphia
Classic look, young.

Daffy Dan's
1126 Dickinson
Elizabeth, N.J.
(201) 352-6931
Major Credit Cards
Other locations: Totowa, N.J.
Their motto is "Clothing bargains for millionaires."
Discounts of 50% or better. High Fashion and Classic
looks.

Feminique
143½ Orchard Street
New York, N.Y.
(212) 475-5392
Major Credit Cards
Great contemporary selection. Lots of sizes. 20%–40%
discounts for primarily High Fashion looks.

Fleisher West
4110 West Lake Street
Minneapolis, Minn.
(612) 927-0466
Major Credit Cards
Better/Designer clothing at 20%–30% discounts. No
seconds. High Fashion and Classic looks.

French Connection
1211 Madison Avenue
New York, N.Y.
(212) 348-4990
Major Credit Cards
Great for separates. Classic styles. 10%–20% above
wholesale.

Importique
16733 Ventura Blvd.
Encino, Calif.
(213) 990-4733
Major Credit Cards
High quality, mostly European imports. 30%–60% below regular retail. High Fashion and Classic looks.

Jay Kay Retail Corp.
141 Orchard Street
New York, N.Y.
(212) 477-3090
Major Credit Cards
More mature, Classic looks.

Le Shop
926 Nicollet Mall
Minneapolis, Minn.
(612) 332-5700
Major Credit Cards
Top American designer's clothing at 20%–50% off of
regular retail prices. Chic discounting. High Fashion
and Classic looks.

Loehmann's
9 West Fordham Road
Bronx, N.Y.
(212) 295-4100
No credit cards; no returns, refunds, or exchanges.
Other locations:
Alabama: Birmingham
Arizona: Phoenix
California: Reseda
           Fullerton
           Los Angeles
           Daly City
           Sunnyvale
Colorado: Denver
Connecticut: Norwalk
             Orange
             Windsor
             Farmington
Florida: Pompano Beach
         North Miami
Georgia: DeKalb City, Atlanta
         Cobb City, Atlanta
Illinois: Morton Grove, Chicago
          Downers Grove, Chicago
          Chicago
Kansas: Overland Park
Maryland: Towson
          Rockville
Massachusetts: Natick
               Swampscott
               Burlington
               Springfield
Michigan: Farmington Hills
Minnesota: Bloomington

New Jersey: Paramus
          East Brunswick
          Pennsauken
          Florham Park
New York: Long Island
          Westchester
North Carolina: Charlotte
          Winston-Salem
          Durham
Ohio: Cincinnati
Pennsylvania: Drexel Hill
          North Wales
          Bethel Park
South Carolina: Charleston
Tennessee: Memphis
Texas: Houston
       Dallas
       Austin
       San Antonio
Virginia: Falls Church
Washington: Seattle
Wisconsin: Milwaukee
Large selection, lots to wade through but good finds.
30%–50% discounts. After that, cycled markdowns.
High Fashion and Classic looks.

New Store
289 Seventh Avenue
New York, N.Y.
(212) 741-1077
Major Credit Cards
Wide selection of designer and young designer looks.
High Fashion and Classic looks. 20%–40% discounts.

Nice Stuff
493 Columbus Avenue
New York, N.Y.
(212) 362-1020
Major Credit Cards
Other locations: East Orange, Union, Chatham, New
Providence, Parsippany, N.J.; Charleston, S.C.; Hal-
landale, Fla.
Their slogan is "Where to afford the clothes you can't
afford." For High Fashion and Classic looks at 50%
discounts.

Noodnick
690 Lexington Avenue
New York, N.Y.
(212) 980-0219
Major Credit Cards
Separates. Contemporary styling for High Fashion
and Classic. 20%–40% discounts.

Peta Lewis
1120 Lexington Avenue
New York, N.Y.
(212) 744-7660
Major Credit Cards
Other locations: Scarsdale, Bronxville, N.Y.; Secau-
cus, N.J.
Designer separates. High Fashion and Classic. 20%–
30% discounts.

Piller's of Eagle Rock
1800 Colorado Blvd.
Eagle Rock, Calif.
(213) 257-8166
Major Credit Cards

All name-brand clothing and shoes at 50% below regular retail. Twice a year a 3-for-1 sale and also a 4-for-1 sale. Caters to all ages, both High Fashion and Classic looks.

Private Collections
230 West 39th Street
New York, N.Y.
(212) 944-0172
Major Credit Cards
Separates from domestic manufacturers bearing Private Collections labels. 50% below regular retail. Strongest on suits. High Fashion and Classic styles.

Putumayo
857 Lexington Avenue
New York, N.Y.
(212) 734-3111
Major Credit Cards
Imported separates. High Fashion styles.

Remin's
665 North Avenue
New Rochelle, N.Y.
(914) 632-3551
All sportswear, coats, dresses, gowns and suits. Prestigious designers. 40%–50% off retail. Helpful, knowledgeable sales help. Spacious, clean store.

S & W
165 West 26th Street
New York, N.Y.
(212) 924-6656
Major Credit Cards
Designer sportswear and dresses at 25%–40% discounts. High Fashion and Classic looks.

Sacks (SFO)
8 Horizon Avenue
Venice, Calif.
(213) 399-8890
Major Credit Cards
Other locations: Culver City
Designer and name brands at 40%–70% below regular retail. All natural fibers, lots of silks, suedes, leathers. High Fashion and Classic looks.

Scandal
1179 Second Avenue
New York, N.Y.
(212) 759-4319
Major Credit Cards
Excellent selection for High Fashion looks.

Shelley's Place
609 Second Avenue
New York, N.Y.
(212) 689-4077
Major Credit Cards
Wide selection of young designer merchandise for High Fashion looks at discounted prices.

Swing Low
1181 Second Avenue
New York, N.Y.
(212) 838-3314
Major Credit Cards
Specializes in hand knit sweaters. Great selection of sportswear for High Fashion and Classic looks.

Symma Inc.
470 Prospect Avenue
West Orange, N.J.
(201) 736-3229
Major Credit Cards
Top designer merchandise, always something on sale. Up to 75% off. High Fashion and Classic styles.

Syms
45 Park Place
New York, N.Y.
(212) 791-1199
Only Syms Card
Other locations: Long Island, Westchester, Buffalo, N.Y.; Bergen County, Woodbridge, N.J.; Falls Church, Rockville, Washington; Norwood, W. Peabody, Massachusetts; Ft. Lauderdale, Fla.
Very large selection. Lots to wade through but some real finds. High Fashion and Classic looks.

Verushka
2077 Broadway
New York, N.Y.
(212) 724-2990
Major Credit Cards
Excellent selection with 25%–50% discounts on designer clothing for High Fashion and Classic looks.

Shopping through mail order is another option. You'll be able to shop at your leisure as well as get a great deal of fashion direction from the many catalogs available. Just write a note requesting a catalog or call the numbers provided below. In most cases, you'll be added to the mailing lists for free. The following are some of the best from which to choose:

Camp Beverly Hills
9615 Brighton Way
Beverly Hills, CA 90210
(800) 323-1717
(800) 942-8881 in Illinois
(213) 202-0069 in California
Major Credit Cards
High Fashion chic active sportswear. Most things bear the "Camp Beverly Hills" logo. Reasonable.

Esprit
800 Minnesota Street
San Francisco, CA 94107
(800) 227-3777
(800) 652-1516 in California
High style activewear and sportswear. Young, contemporary. Most items made from natural fibers. Great prices, high quality.

Honeybee
2745 Philmont Avenue
Huntingdon Valley, Pa. 19006
(800) 523-6534
(215) 947-8080 in Pennsylvania.
Major Credit Cards
Traditional with some High Fashion. Emphasis on accessories. Many coordinating outfits.

The Horchow Collection
4435 Simonton
Dallas, TX 75234
(800) 527-0303
(800) 442-5806
Major Credit Cards
Traditional, contemporary styling in active sportswear, separates, dresses, etc. Many clothes are Horchow exclusives.

L. L. Bean
Freeport, ME 04033
(207) 865-3111 (24 hrs.)
Major Credit Cards
One of the most prestigious catalogs among the rich with Classic tastes. Large selection of knit and oxford shirts, sweaters, slacks, etc. All at good prices.

Land's End
Lands End Lane
Dodgeville, WI 53533
(800) 356-4444
(608) 935-2788 in Wisconsin
Major Credit Cards
Classic sportswear at extremely reasonable prices.

Laura Ashley
Mail Order Department
55 Triangle Blvd.
Carlstadt, NJ 07072
Major Credit Cards
Separates, dresses and nightgowns in distinctive floral prints. The simple country look with Victorian collars. Classic yet High Fashion in styling.

Peachtree Report
4795 Fulton Industrial Blvd.
Atlanta, GA 30336
(800) 241-9321
(404) 691-7633 in Georgia
Designer and young designer styles. Traditional looks for all ages. More suburban than city sophisticated.

Spiegel
P.O. Box 927
Oak Brook, ILL 60521
(312) 986-1088
Extremely good selection of designer and name-brand merchandise for High Fashion and Classic looks.

Sportpages
3373 Towerwood Drive
Dallas, TX 75234
(800) 527-3166
(214) 484-8900 in Texas
Major Credit Cards
Active sportswear, dresses, sweaters, etc. Traditional styling.